Hedgehogs

CONTENTS

Introduction 2

What do hedgehogs look like? 4

How do hedgehogs live?. 8

Helping hedgehogs 14

Index 16

Introduction

Hedgehogs are wild animals. They can...

roll into a ball

climb walls

build nests

swim

dig for food

What do hedgehogs look like?

Hedgehogs have short thin legs and a very short tail.

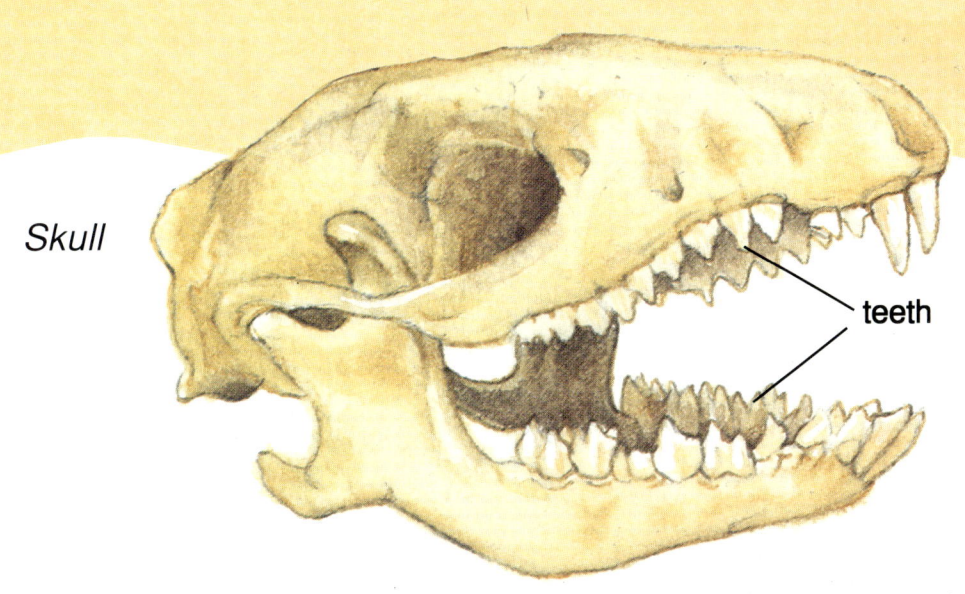

They have sharp teeth.

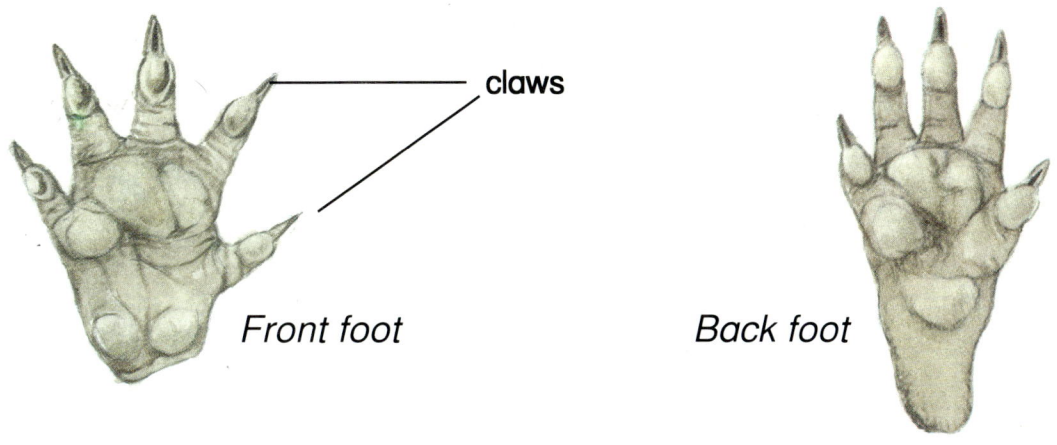

Hedgehogs have five long, sharp claws on each foot.

Close-up of prickles

A hedgehog uncurling

Hedgehogs have prickles on their backs.
When they are frightened they roll into a ball.
The prickles keep other animals away.

Hedgehogs have bright eyes but they *cannot* see very well.

Hedgehogs have small noses but they *can* smell very well.

How do hedgehogs live?

Hedgehogs sleep in the winter and wake in the spring. They **hibernate.**

Hedgehogs sleep during the day and wake in the evening. They are **nocturnal.**

Hedgehogs make their nests under hedges or near walls. They like quiet places.

Hedgehog babies are called **piglets.**
The piglets are born blind and have soft prickles.

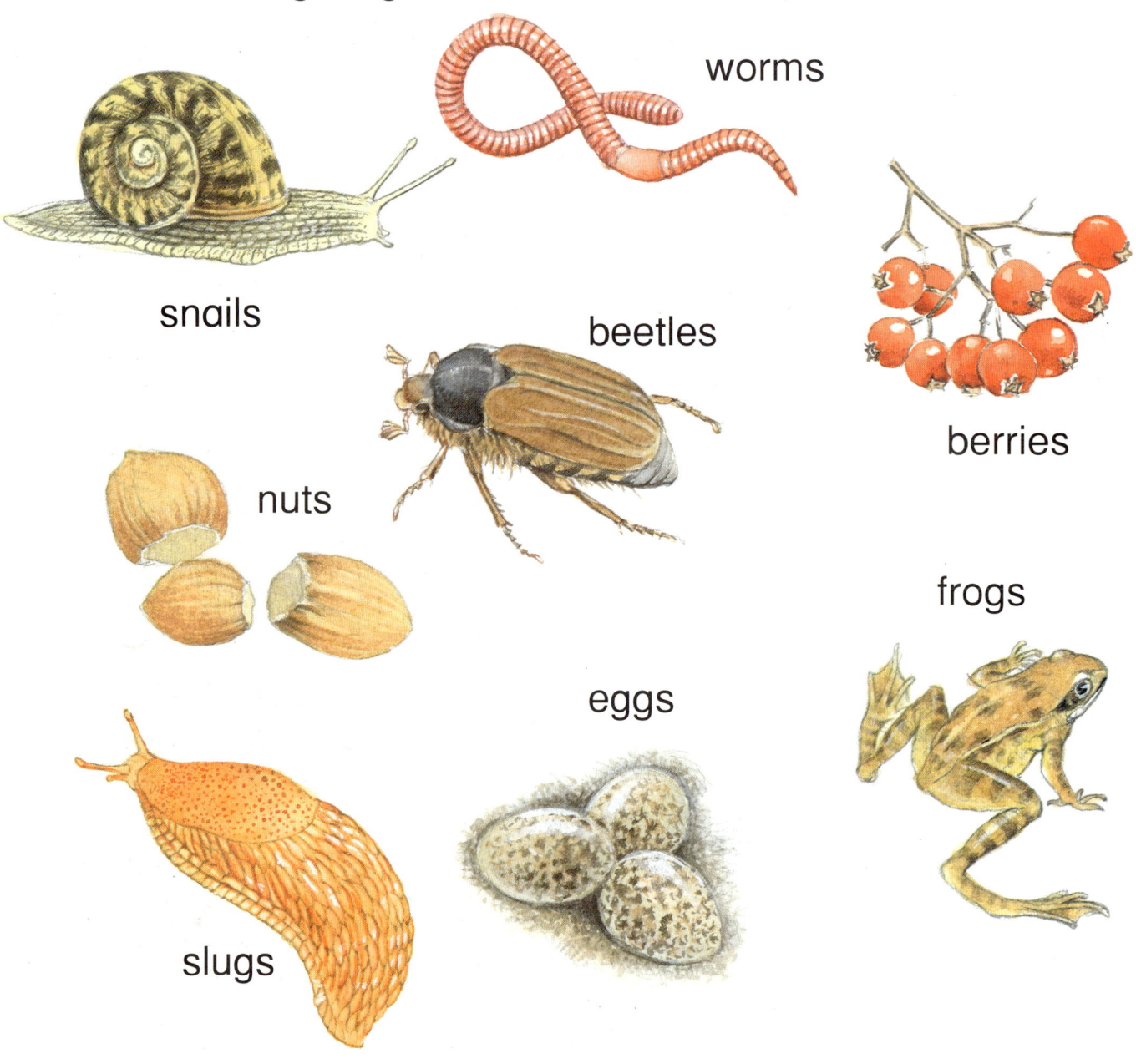

Hedgehogs look for food in the evenings. Some people leave food out for hedgehogs.

cat food

Helping hedgehogs

People help hedgehogs in other ways.

Feeding a baby hedgehog

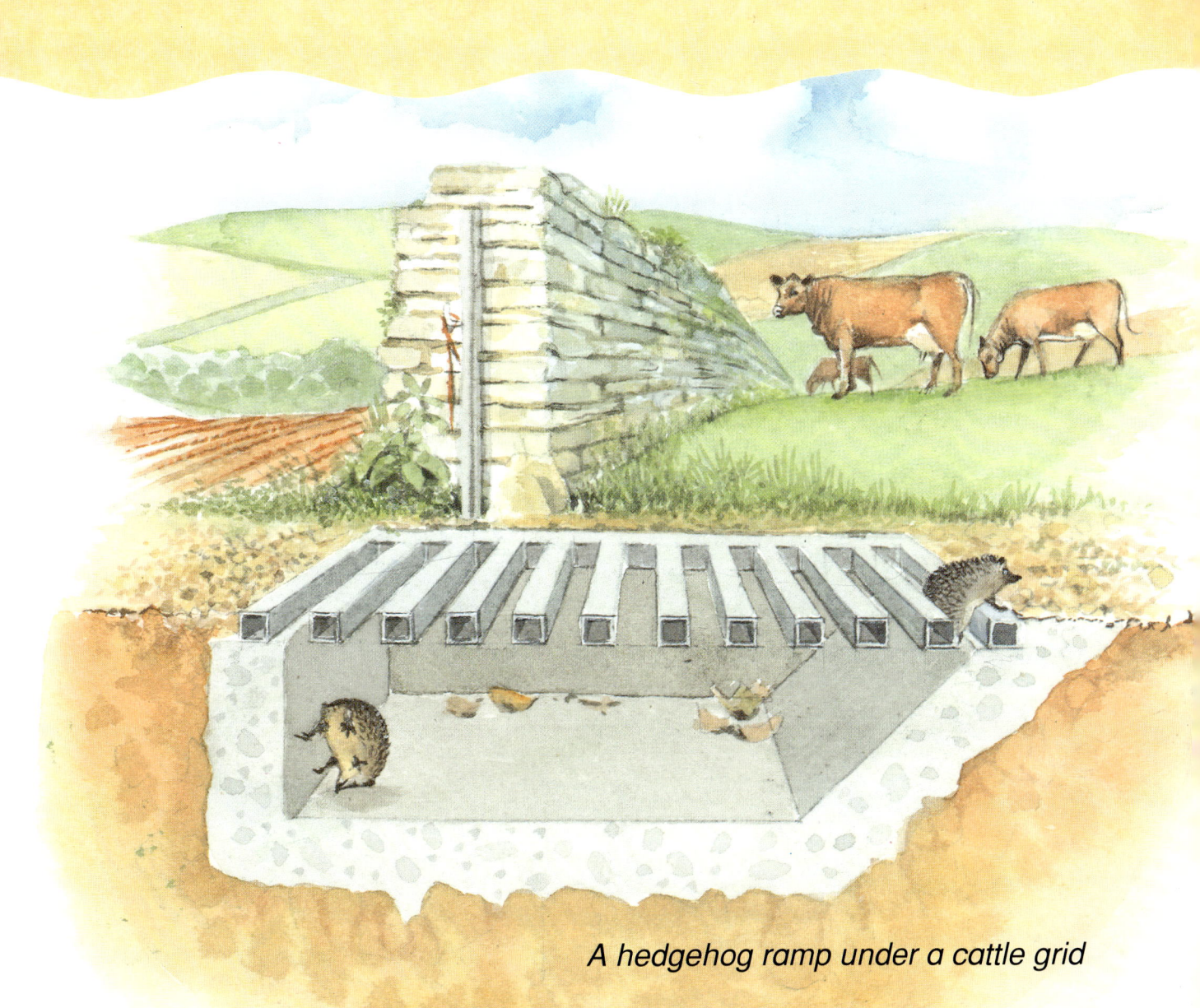

A hedgehog ramp under a cattle grid

Index

babies 11

claws 5

eyes 7

food 13

legs 4

nest 10

nose 7

piglets 11

prickles 6, 11

tail 4

teeth 5